Steve Parish KIDS

Nature watch Mammals

CONTENTS

What makes me a mammal?

Koala

Girl with joey

You may not think that you are much like a kangaroo, an echidna or a seal, but you share one thing that is the same — you are all mammals. Mammals are covered with fur or hair that helps them stay warm.

Sea-lions

Bottlenose dolphin

Milk from Mum

All mammals, even seals and dolphins, feed their babies on milk that the mothers produce. They also have fine hairs that cover their bodies.

Dingoes

I drink milk, just like you!

Baby possum

Most mammals give birth to live babies. Sometimes the babies are born without hair, but it quickly grows and covers their bodies.

Fur

A special type of hair

Even the spiky, spiny echidna is a mammal. Its spines are just a special type of hair. Special differences like this help animals survive and are called adaptations.

Echidna spines

Different kinds of mammals

There are three different mammal groups — placental mammals (like you), monotremes (like the echidna and platypus) and marsupial mammals (like kangaroos).

Striped possum

Bats

Dingo

Sea-lion

PLACENTAL mammals, like you, bats, dingoes and seals, have live young. They don't have pouches or lay eggs.

It doesn't matter whether a baby mammal grows in its mum's belly, grows in a pouch or hatches from an egg, the mother still feeds it milk. Drinking milk is another thing that sets mammals apart from other animals.

Platypus

Koala & baby

We all **grow** differently as babies.

Echidna

Grey kangaroo & joey

MONOTREMES, like the platypus and echidna, lay eggs.

MARSUPIAL mammals, like koalas, kangaroos and gliders, have pouches.

Egg-laying mammals

Echidna

Monotremes (egg-laying mammals) are very odd animals. The only monotremes in the world are echidnas and the platypus. This makes Australia the best place to study these amazing mammals.

Platypus

Puggle

Baby platypuses drink milk differently to other mammals. Small patches of skin on the mother platypus's belly ooze milk and wet her fur. The young platypuses suck their mother's fur to drink the milk. Platypuses live in the water and have three layers of thick fur to help them stay dry.

A platypus's eggs are very small — smaller than half the size of a twenty cent piece.

Perfect little puggles

Baby echidnas are called puggles. They are born without any spines. Soon after they hatch, soft hair grows. The spines appear when they are older.

Look but don't touch

Echidna spines are very sharp. They help echidnas avoid being eaten by their enemies. The spines can also hurt you if you touch them. It is best not to touch wild creatures at all unless you are with a wildlife carer at a fauna park.

Pouched mammals

Wombat

Australia has a lot of marsupials, which are mammals that grow their babies in pouches.

When a marsupial is born, it has no hair and is as tiny as a jelly bean! It crawls up into its mother's cosy pouch, where it drinks milk, grows hair and gets bigger.

Months later, when it is too big for the pouch, it clings on to its mother's fur or starts to move about on its own.

Baby koala

Koalas

Baby ringtail possums

Pocket pouches

Bandicoots have pouches that face backwards, so dirt won't get in the "pocket" when the mother bandicoot digs for food. The picture on the left shows a baby trying to get into its mum's pouch, but it is too big to fit.

Brown bandicoot & joey

Grey kangaroo & joey

Albino red-necked wallaby & joey

Marsupials come in many colours, sometimes even pure white, like the albino wallaby above. But a white mother may not always pass on its colour to its baby.

Watch out for baby

It is fun to watch and photograph kangaroos at your local wildlife park, but if a kangaroo has a baby joey in its pouch you should be careful not to get too close.

Belly-button mammals

Fur-seal

You belong to a group of mammals known as placental mammals.

A baby placental mammal doesn't live in a pouch. Instead it grows bigger inside its mother's tummy.

Dingo

Inside the mother, the baby is attached to a special sac called a placenta. The placenta takes food and oxygen from the mother's blood and passes these to the baby through a tube called an umbilical cord.

Baby bats

Babies left behind

Bats are placental mammals. Some of the mothers give birth to babies at around the same time. The babies are then left in a big group while the mothers go off hunting for food to bring back to their babies.

Bat

We are belly-button mammals too!

Bottlenose dolphins

just like you

You can tell where your umbilical cord used to be because it now forms your belly button. All placental mammals have a belly button, just like you do.

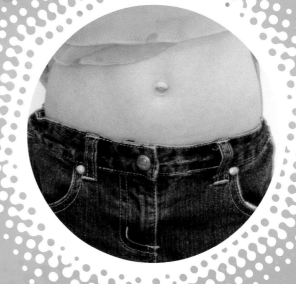

Tasmanian devil

The great Australian bite

Scientists can tell which type of mammal an animal is from the shape of its skull, jaws and teeth, as well as how it gives birth to its young.

A mammal's teeth and jaws suit the type of food it eats. Teeth made for biting are known as incisors or "canine teeth" and are sharp and pointed. Teeth made for grinding and chewing are further back in the cheek and are called molars.

Koala teeth

Wombats and koalas are plant eaters. Their front teeth can snip off even the toughest of plants.

The most teeth

The numbat has the most teeth of all mammals. It has 52 teeth, but it doesn't really need them because it eats only termites, which are very soft.

Numbat

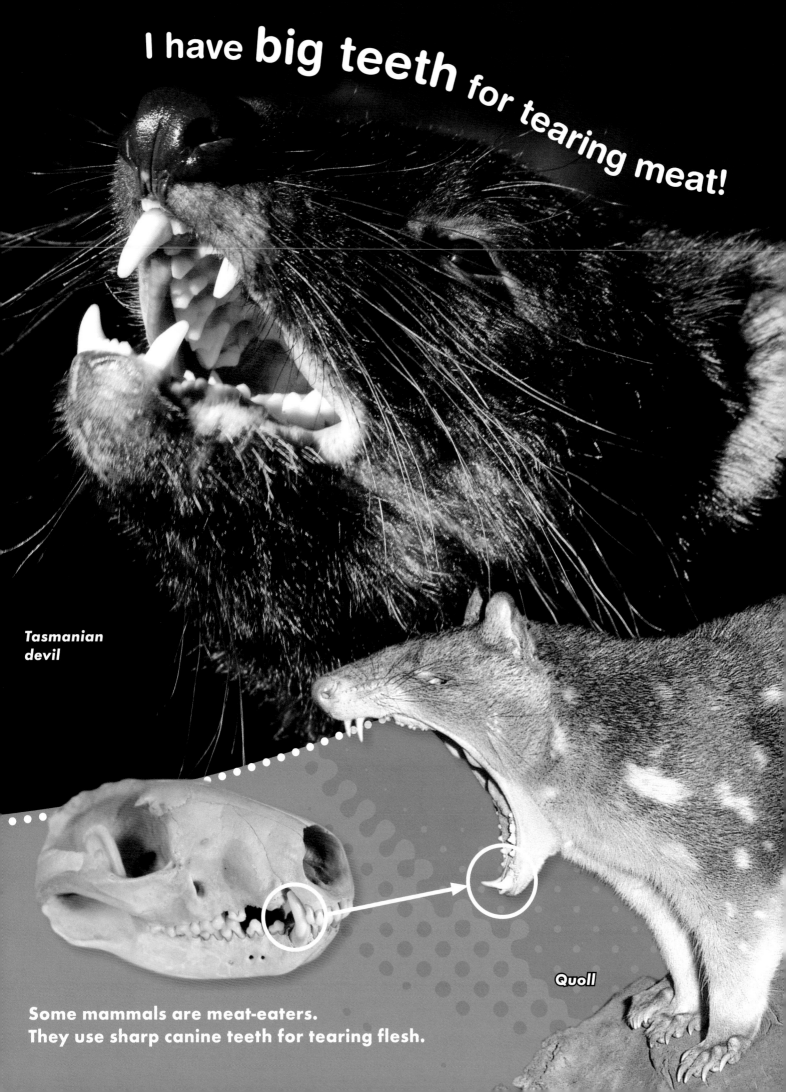

I have big teeth for tearing meat!

Tasmanian devil

Quoll

Some mammals are meat-eaters.
They use sharp canine teeth for tearing flesh.

Different dinners

Mulgara

Tasmanian devil

Like humans, many mammals eat meat, as well as vegetables, leaves, nectar or fruit. These mammals are called omnivores. Some small desert mammals also get all the water they need from food like insects and leaves.

Meat-eating animals like the Tasmanian devil and the dunnart are called carnivores. They catch and kill their own food or sniff out dead animals that have been killed by something else, which is called scavenging.

Dunnart

Sea Cows

Another special kind of mammal lives in the sea and is called a dugong. Dugongs eat only seagrass. For this reason they are sometimes known as "sea cows". Other marine mammals, such as seals and sea-lions, eat fish. Whales eat tiny shrimp-like animals called krill.

Dugong

We are herbivores. We eat plants.

Koalas

Koalas and greater gliders are herbivores, which means they only eat plants. They eat gum leaves and they are very fussy, choosing them from only a few types of gum tree.

Greater glider

Herbivore or Carnivore?

If you eat vegetables and meat then you are an omnivore. Some people choose to eat only vegetables and do not eat meat at all. They are known as "vegetarians", which is another name for herbivores.

15

Moving like a mammal

All mammals have a backbone, which is made up of lots of small bones to make it bend. Your skeleton is also supported by a backbone, called your spine, which protects your spinal cord.

You are only able to walk, run, jump and play because your brain sends messages to your muscles, which are all connected to a hard skeleton beneath your skin.

For a hopping-mouse to move around its desert home, its brain must first send messages to its spine and muscles. Its bones, like yours, have joints that give the hopping-mouse the flexibility to run, jump, leap and groom its fur.

Hopping-mouse

A bony skeleton

A mammal's skeleton may differ slightly to suit its lifestyle, but it remains mostly the same. Even mammals that hop, swim or fly all have skeletons and backbones, although the size of the bones may change.

Bandicoot skeleton

16

Bones under my skin help me move...

We all move the same

The spinal cord carries messages from your brain to your muscles. When your muscles get the message, they move and your bones move with them! Mammals, like these young brushtail possums, all move in this way.

17

Glider

Up, up & away

Bats are the only true flying mammals. All other airborne mammals are really only gliding. The difference is that bats are able to flap their wings, like birds do. Gliders do not flap.

Flying-fox

Gliders have a membrane of skin that connects to each arm and stretches to the ankle. A glider's "wings" look more square than a bat's. Wind beneath the membrane helps gliders to soar from one tree to another but they cannot "fly" long distances like bats do.

Featherless fliers

Unlike birds, bats do not have feathers to help them fly. Instead, their wings are made up of a thin layer of stretchy skin called a membrane.

Little red flying-foxes

Ghost bats

Amazingly, I can fly with my fingers!

The long bones that stretch to the wing tips are the bat's fingers. The bat's hands are circled in the photograph below.

Give me five!

Can you see the bat's wrist above?

Can you find the bat's fingers and thumb?

Hop to it!

Kangaroos

The most famous hoppers are kangaroos and wallabies, but some other small mammals, such as hopping-mice, also move in this way.

Kangaroos and other hopping mammals have very large back leg muscles and tendons that act like powerful, elastic springs. Their big feet are attached to these muscles and tendons and together they work like a slingshot to help the animal hop.

When you hop you get puffed easily because your body is not designed for hopping. (Try it!) But hopping is an adaptation that helps some other mammals save energy! A kangaroo's body even uses less oxygen to hop than to run.

Red-necked pademelon

Bridled nailtail wallaby

No going back...

Kangaroos and hopping-mice cannot go backwards because they have to move both of their back legs at the same time to bound. The long, strong tail helps them balance as they hop.

20   Hopping-mouse

My big feet help me hop!

Red kangaroo

How far can you jump?

A red kangaroo can jump several metres in a single bound. How high and how far can you jump in a single leap?

Making sense of life

Pademelon

You use sight, smell, touch, taste and hearing to help you explore your world, and other mammals do too. Their senses help them "make sense" of their surroundings. How and where a mammal lives decides what senses it needs to use most.

Prowling meat-eaters, like dingoes and quolls, need a good sense of sight, smell and hearing to find and catch prey. Shy bandicoots and kangaroos have good eyesight, hearing and smell because they need to be able to escape from their enemies.

Barred bandicoot

Flying-fox

Have you ever heard the saying, "as blind as a bat"? Well, if you have, it's not true. Bats and flying-foxes are not blind at all. In fact, most mammals have good eyesight.

Seal whiskers

For many mammals, whiskers are important for sensing the environment around them. Seals have very sensitive whiskers, which can be used to feel for fish in dark or murky waters.

Cuscus

Platypus

I have a special sixth sense!

Platypus

Your five senses

Hearing, seeing, touching, tasting and smelling are your five senses, but mammals often use sight and smell more than the others. Some people may have lost one of these senses, making them blind or deaf. Often, this makes another sense even stronger. Sometimes we forget that we are sensing the world around us all of the time.

The platypus has small eyes but good sight and hearing. It only opens its eyes when it is above water and is very good at spotting movement on the river bank. Little is known about its sense of smell and taste, but scientists do know it has a special sixth sense called electroreception. It uses electroreceptors in its sensitive bill to find food under water, when its eyes are closed.

23

Hear, hear!

You probably cannot move your ears (although some people can wiggle theirs!), but kangaroos and bilbies can. They swivel their ears to face the direction of a noise. Hearing is important for most mammals, whether they live on land or in the sea.

Flying-fox

Flying-foxes have excellent hearing. This helps them to fly away at the first sound of danger.

Some mammals, such as seals, dolphins, platypuses and echidnas, have only very tiny earholes that are very hard to see. Animals with such small ears mostly have other, more important ways of sensing their surroundings.

Red kangaroo

Fur-seal & pup

Ears that cool blood

The bilby's big ears don't just help it avoid danger, they also help keep it cool! Bilbies live in hot places where it is important to stay cool. Their big ears are filled with small veins. The air outside cools the blood in these veins as it flows through the bilby's large ears.

Bilby

I hear an echo, echo, echo...

Bottlenose dolphin

Listening to echoes

One of the strangest ways to hear is by echolocation. Whales, dolphins and bats use echolocation, which is listening to echoes. This style of hearing helps them understand the shape of their surroundings because they are "listening" to the echoes that bounce off objects around them.

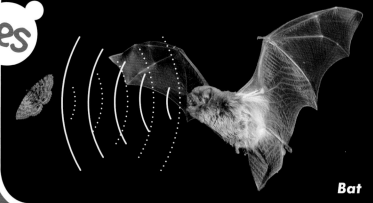

Bat

What's that pong?

Koala

What is your favourite smell? Perfume? Breakfast? Roses? Like you, most land mammals are able to smell food, flowers and the "scent" given off by other animals. They can also sniff out smoke in the air and predators, which helps them to avoid danger.

Dingoes

This picture shows dingoes picking up the scent of another dog, which left its smell by peeing on the ground, logs and trees.

Some mammals even have special scent patches (known as glands) that they use to mark their territory or to attract a mate. Male koalas have a sticky patch on their chests (seen in the picture opposite). They rub the patch against trees to leave smelly "messages" for other koalas that might visit the area.

Musky rat-kangaroo

A little stinker

The musky rat-kangaroo lives in the rainforests of north Queensland and is named for its funny, musky smell. Scientists do not know why it gives off such a strong pong.

Male koala

I can smell messages left by others.

Wombat poo

The wombat does not have scent glands like its relative the koala. Instead, the males mark their home territory by pooing on top of a rock.

Who "nose" what the nose knows?

Wombat nose

Mammals' noses have many shapes and sizes. Whether round like a wombat's or long and thin like an echidna's, their shape and size can tell you how mammals sniff out their food. Mammals also often use their noses for more than just smelling.

Wombats have a great sense of smell. A wombat's blunt, rubbery nose is also used for nudging soil out of the way when it digs its burrow under the ground.

Some mammal mothers recognise their young by their scent. This is important when mothers have to leave their young to find food for them. The baby's smell helps its mother find it quickly when she returns.

Wallaby & joey

Snuffle snouts

Brown bandicoot

Barred bandicoot

Bandicoots poke their long snouts into the earth to "snuffle" out worms and insects hidden in the soil.

Some bats have strange-shaped noses that include fleshy "noseleaves". These funny flaps of skin help them echolocate, which is listening to echoes, much like whales and dolphins do (see page 25).

Orange leaf-nosed bat

Platypus

feeling nosey?

Noses can be very sensitive. The echidna presses its nose against fallen logs to "feel" for termites inside. The platypus's nose is very sensitive to touch and is used to find food under the water by sensing weak electrical signals from swimming animals, like crayfish and tadpoles, as well as other prey.

Echidna

Psst, get over here!

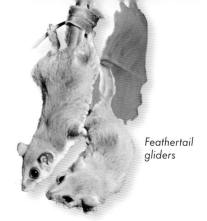

Feathertail gliders

Mammals communicate with each other in many ways. They may use smell, make sounds, or use certain behaviours to show fear, to comfort or just say "hello". Even the way they hold their bodies or move can act as a "language" between mammals of the same kind.

Bennett's wallabies

Some kangaroos and wallabies thump their tails as an alarm call if they are upset or threatened. This warns the rest of the mob, or group, that there is danger.

Adult wallabies "talk" to each other mainly through "body language", but mothers may also make soft clicks and clucks to their joeys.

Red-necked wallabies

Grooming is one way that animals look after each other. Friendly mammals may lick each other's fur, nuzzle each other, or pick burrs and ticks from each other's coats.

We hoooOOOowwwwwllllll...

Koala

Bellows & howls

Male koalas "yell out" to other males and females during the mating season by making a loud snoring sound called a bellow.

If you have a dog, it probably barks from time to time. Dingoes are native dogs, but they never bark; they only howl. Howling is a way of "talking" to other dingoes.

31

Singers & Chatterboxes

Sperm whales

Are you a good singer? Whales certainly are. They "talk" to other whales by singing. In fact, whales are such good singers they may have hundreds of songs.

Whale watching

In some places around Australia, you can go on a whale-watching boat ride to see these magnificent mammals.

Dolphins have also developed an unusual language. They use many clicks and sounds to "talk" to each other.

Dolphins

Whale songs may be up to ten minutes long and, depending on the species, may include roars, clicks, sighs, moans, trumpets and squeals. Songs are also used to help whales find their way, or navigate, in the ocean.

We can sing, sigh and click under water.

Whales sing songs, but they don't have vocal chords like humans do, so scientists aren't sure how they make these noises!

Fighting for food or fun

Tasmanian devils

Sometimes humans have arguments and mammals are no different. Mammals may fight over food, over territory, or over partners. Some fighting is even just for play.

Kangaroos are famous for their boxing skills. Male kangaroos fight to see who will be the leader of the "mob". They not only box with their front paws, they may also kick with their strong back legs.

Male red kangaroos

Dingo

Red kangaroo

Some animals choose not to fight at all, but rather to run or hide to avoid any danger. An echidna rolls itself up into a tight spiky ball or digs straight down into the ground to avoid attack.

Echidna

Tasmanian devils and dingoes fight fiercely over food. The best fighter usually gets the most dinner, so it really is survival of the toughest! Young Tasmanian devils and dingoes also "play fight", which helps them learn the skills they need as adults.

Sea-lions

Roaring Wrestlers

Male seals and sea-lions fight by roaring, wrestling and biting each other. They fight to make sure they get the most females, which stay with the male in a group called a harem.

Home is where the heart is...

Mammals can live in many different environments, including the tree tops, the deserts, the oceans and even underground.

Rock-wallabies

Rock-wallabies are amazing leapers. They make large bounds from rock to rock in the habitats in which they live. Tough soles on their feet and large tails help rock-wallabies balance.

Native mice and bandicoots make cosy nests of straw and grasses, where they can hide from predators.

Native mice

Brown bandicoots

36

I have a special home in the trees.

Tree-kangaroo

Climbing kangaroos!

Tree-kangaroos live high up in the forest under a thick layer, or canopy, of tree branches. The canopy is like the "roof" of the rainforest. You would need to be an excellent climber to find a tree-kangaroo.

Life in a hollow or burrow

Bettong

Do you like to play in a cubby house? So do many Australian mammals. Some spend most of their lives safe and secure in a hollow log or tree. Many give birth to their babies in these tree-hollow shelters and sleep there. When trees are cut down, these animals might lose their homes! Others are great diggers that build comfortable underground tunnels.

Wombat

Wombats are wonderful diggers. They have powerful legs and sharp claws for scratching out deep burrows.

Wombat claws

Bilbies make their homes in the desert where they dig burrows to live in. During the heat of the day they stay cool below ground. At night they come out to feed on seeds and grasses.

Bilbies

Ringtail possums

We need hollow logs to live in.

Tree-hollow homes

It takes a long time for a tree to grow big enough to have a hollow that animals, like bats and possums, can use as a home. Some tree hollows might be a hundred years old or even more!

Bats

Life under water

Even though you don't live in the water, you can learn to swim using your arms and legs to stroke and kick.

Platypus

Many other mammals swim in a similar way. Even waddling echidnas and climbing koalas can swim! But some mammals spend almost their entire lives swimming in the ocean, creeks or streams.

Water-rat

Platypuses and water-rats are excellent swimmers. They can swim either on the surface or under the water, where they chase and eat crayfish.

Fur-seal

Can you float?

Sea mammals like fur-seals have other adaptations for life at sea. Beneath a sea mammal's tough skin is a layer of fat called blubber. Blubber keeps the animal warm and helps it float. When snorkelling with mum or dad, see if you can float like a sea mammal.

My flippers help me swim fast.

Whales, dolphins, seals and sea-lions spend most of their lives swimming. Beneath their slippery skins, they have skeletons very like your own, but their hands and feet are paddle-shaped flippers to help them swim. Imagine how fast you could swim if you had flippers on your hands and your feet!

Blowhole boogers

Whales and dolphins spend their whole lives swimming, but they must come up to the surface regularly to breathe air. A whale has just one "nostril" to breathe through — its blowhole. When a whale breathes out, it blows air and "snot" out of its nostril.

Whales

SOCIAL MAMMALS

Safety in numbers

Ringtail possums

Just as lots of people live together in neighbourhoods, many other mammals also live together in groups. They do this because it's safer and easier to communicate and raise young.

Seals and sea-lions live together in noisy colonies on rocky or sandy seashores. Some "babysitting" mothers look after the seal pups while the rest of the mother seals hunt.

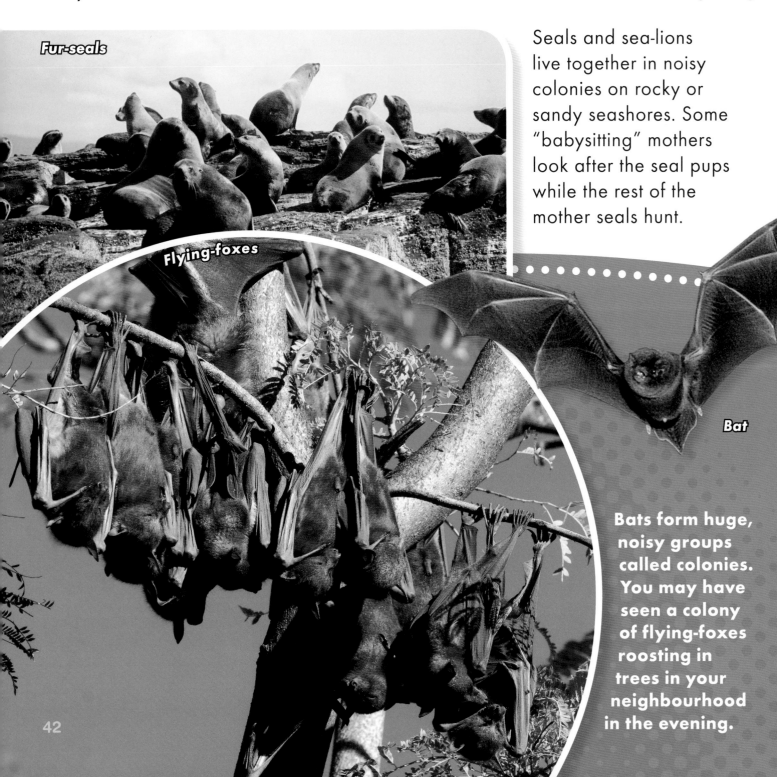

Fur-seals

Flying-foxes

Bat

Bats form huge, noisy groups called colonies. You may have seen a colony of flying-foxes roosting in trees in your neighbourhood in the evening.

Grey kangaroos

Kangaroos live together in mobs to help protect themselves from dingoes. Some of the kangaroos keep watch for danger and alert their friends if threats are near.

Koalas

You probably would not feel safe in the bush on your own and many mammals feel exactly the same way. Just like you and your family, many mammals feel safe when their family and friends are close by.

Koalas prefer to live alone and each koala has its own territory. But koala neighbourhoods often have some shared trees where they find mates and "hang out" with other koalas.

43

Daytime is playtime

Grey kangaroos

Many mammals eat by day and sleep at night. Others sleep by day and eat and mate at night. Some may be active either day or night, depending on the weather and season.

Some mammals like to be out at dawn and in the evening around sunset. They prefer to sleep or hide for the rest of the day and late at night.

Numbat

Daytime animals

Some day-active, or diurnal, mammals are echidnas, numbats and the musky rat-kangaroo. Several kangaroo and wallaby species also come out to feed in the early morning or at dusk.

Echidna

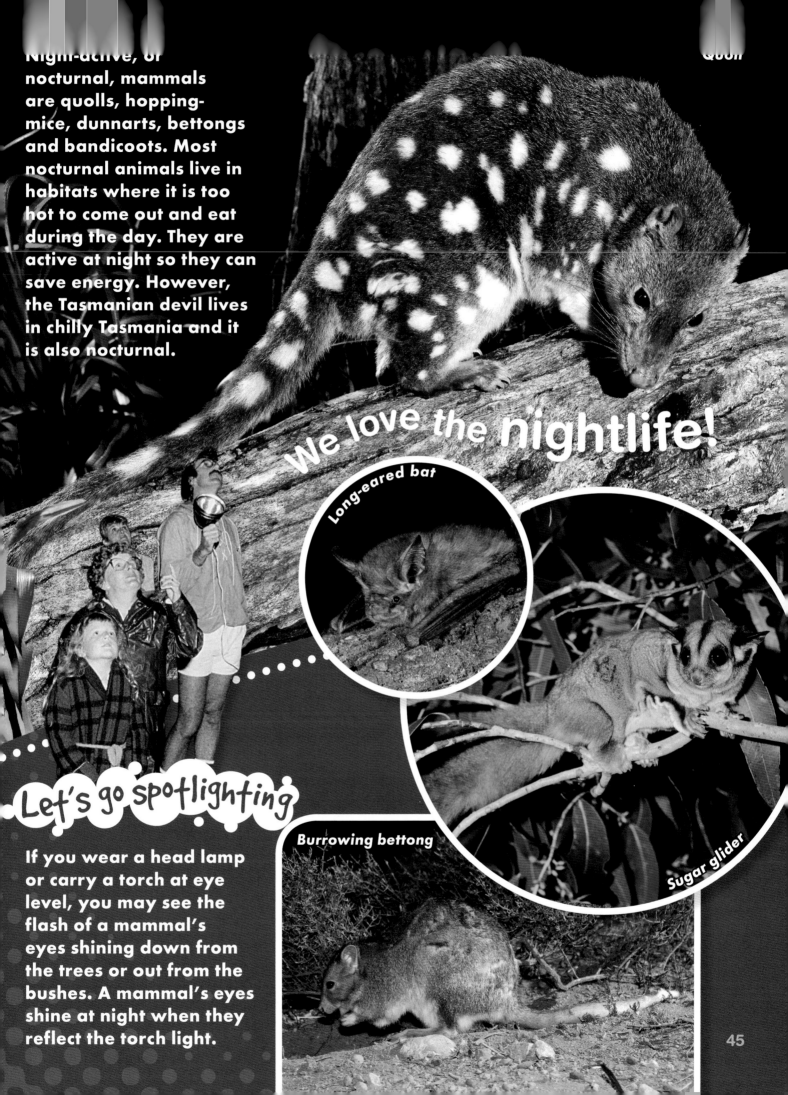

Night-active, or nocturnal, mammals are quolls, hopping-mice, dunnarts, bettongs and bandicoots. Most nocturnal animals live in habitats where it is too hot to come out and eat during the day. They are active at night so they can save energy. However, the Tasmanian devil lives in chilly Tasmania and it is also nocturnal.

Quoll

We love the nightlife!

Long-eared bat

Let's go spotlighting

If you wear a head lamp or carry a torch at eye level, you may see the flash of a mammal's eyes shining down from the trees or out from the bushes. A mammal's eyes shine at night when they reflect the torch light.

Burrowing bettong

Sugar glider

45

Caring about mammals

Quoll

Some Australian mammals are at risk because their habitats are changing. Changes to our environment are happening very quickly. We are clearing or polluting land and scientists do not think animals will be able to adapt quickly enough. Animals become extinct when there are no animals of that kind left alive. Animals at risk of extinction are said to be endangered.

The rare mahogany glider is endangered. Like the koala, it eats only gum leaves. If its home and food trees are destroyed, it could become extinct.

The tiny mountain pygmy-possum lives in a small, cold part of the Australian Alps, where snow falls in winter. It is endangered because the weather is getting hotter, so its snowy home is shrinking.

Mahogany glider

Mountain pygmy-possum

Bilbies are endangered in the wild. Scientists breed them and then release them in safe areas where there are no cats or dogs.

Bilby

You can help us survive.

Southern hairy-nosed wombat

Numbat

The numbat is the only one of its kind and lives in just a small part of Western Australia.

The southern hairy-nosed wombat is endangered, along with its cousin the northern hairy-nosed wombat.

Numbat

GLOSSARY

ADAPTATIONS Special features that help animals survive.

AIRBORNE To move in the air.

ALBINO An animal that is born without pigment, causing the skin and fur to be white and the eyes pink.

AVOID To keep away from.

CARNIVORE An animal that eats meat and other animals.

CATAPULT To move really quickly.

DESIGNED Made for a special purpose.

DIURNAL An animal that is active during the day.

ECHOLOCATION To sense an object by sending out sounds then listening to the echoes that bounce back off the object.

ELECTRORECEPTION Being able to feel very slight electrical currents.

ENDANGERED At risk of becoming extinct.

EXTINCT When all individuals of a species are dead.

FAUNA Animals.

GROOM To clean and tidy fur.

HABITAT The place where an animal or plant lives or grows.

HAREM A group of females that are protected by a single male.

HERBIVORE An animal that eats plants.

MATE When a male animal transfers special cells to a female's eggs, which causes young ones to develop.

MEMBRANE Thin connective tissue, like the tissue of a bat's wings.

MOB A group of kangaroos or wallabies.

NOCTURNAL An animal that hunts at night.

OMNIVORE An animal that eats both plants and animals.

PLACENTA A sac in placental animals that connects the bloodstream of an unborn animal to its mother.

PREDATOR An animal that hunts and eats animals.

RARE Not common.

REFLECT To show light back.

SCAVENGER An animal that eats dead animals.

SPECIES A group of organisms that are the same type and can breed to make babies.

TENDONS Bands of tough tissue that connect a muscle with a bone and play an important part in helping animals to move.

TERRITORY The area occupied by and defended by an animal or group of animals.

UMBILICAL CORD The tube that connects the baby that is developing inside its mother's tummy to the placenta and allows food and oxygen to be passed from mother to baby.